# Face Book /
# The 2nd Chapter /
# The Architect

Historian Brother Kelly, Tavares Montez

ISBN 979-8-88832-000-6 (paperback)
ISBN 979-8-88832-001-3 (digital)



Christian Faith Publishing
832 Park Avenue
Meadville, PA 16335
www.christianfaithpublishing.com

Printed in the United States of America

# Concerning This Book

My goal here is to capture the essence of salvation through Christian service as a technician.

# Introduction

This is a book of opening and closing chapters in a young man's life concerning the calling of creation, which he is sworn to protect and restore here in America. Using the title of Broken Arrow, the author attempts to clean and repair the foundation of a country that is engaged in war. Prophecies of destruction and chaos behind a world torn by powerful lords that have forgotten the sacred values of the earth's keeper are the main focus of the writer's format. Using the Holy Scripture, from Elder Moses to Father Abraham, the writer attempts to return the world to Christ. May the Holy Father bless the readers of this book.

## A Second introduction

Greetings! This collection of writings are based on African American history as a young male striving in a "Land of Opportunity." Mostly creative writing bridging the gap of nature versus man's trials and tribulations against forces that challenge human nature and our survival as living souls, here in Alabama near the "Jones Valley trail," where many have lost their lives searching for what only heaven knows. In this collection, I, as Broken Arrow, manage to survive the onslaught of verbal attacks. Most of this writing is twenty-first century based on ancient building principles in a land of opportunity and freedom, before and after slavery was an issue. Native African American roots, "The Adventures of Broken Arrow."

# ℭhe Arrow Smith

> Aluminum alloy
> Quick mercury fixes
> Strong fibers
> That bend
> And not break
> Soaked in venom

I awoke early this morning for breakfast. I'm not sure how long these days of mine will last. It is important that I finish this piece. Poverty and destruction are two forces we must be mindful of during our stay here. A journey home is what I call this collection of vibes.

Here I have some pivotal elements of His Holy Word to man through the written word of his holy scripture, concerning the crucifixion of his son. The Lord was crucified and resurrected to deliver a world from sin, hell and death. A world without hope versus the blessings of paradise, something I believe belongs to those deemed worthy of its blessing more abundantly. During my experience here in Alabama, I have come to believe that the legend is a pure element of faith and hope granted to those faithful followers who trust in the ways of righteousness and uphold the practices written in this document. In a land of freedom and liberty, where the American Dream is something all men and women of the faith should be able to reach.

As a student, I learned that building in a spiritual sense is very important to the survival and protection of a species. Its doors and windows, with bars and strong locks, prevent the strongman from entering without permission, special topics like keys to unlock doors to precious treasure, rest for rejuvenating properties and experiences, protection from harsh weather, and conduct considered unfit for a gentleman can all make good sense when we follow the prescription. Lessons we have learned throughout history from our forefathers and the hardships they had to face help us as a generation to achieve a moral victory of faith. Here let us come to grips with what we have to do as individuals to maintain a level of persistence and perseverance in a faith that supports our survival as a people and a nation.

The importance of our work as adults and our ability to give good gifts to our faithful responsibilities as a strong family unit make up the fabric of a great nation, state or community. The excellence and experience of the individual are also important factors. Earlier, I spoke of Father Abraham and how he found God in his lifetime. The Lord promised Abram the land of Canaan as a gift for his belief and a resting place for his offspring.

Elder Moses, the author of the book Genesis, knew the lineage and recorded historical presentations of a people saved by grace. His works in Egypt, recorded in earlier chapters of Genesis, came centuries or generations after Brother Joseph and the famine.

## Harsh Dry Ground

In this book, Adam, defined in the Bible cyclopedia index meaning, "red earth," was challenged by the trees of the garden. He was given the gift of original woman and paradise as a blessing from the creator. The tree of life was a gift to the couple. Another tree in the midst of the garden, the tree of Knowledge, ripe with the fruit of good and evil was there. Something the Holy Father asked them not to eat was there. Entertained by the voice of the serpent they ate the fruit. Sin and disobedience entered into the world and thereby death. Soon after their fall from paradise, prayer and worship entered into the world as a practice of praise and repentance. As curious souls we sometimes worship what we know not. Other deities that the inhabitants worshiped caused the children of Israel to go into captivity.

with a strong hand, they were delivered and became possessors of heaven and earth.

Here, the tree of life comes to mind, the first sign of human development and the Holy Father's relationship with his son, Jesus Christ. The sacred duty of the young man was to restore humanity to its rightful luster, like a jewel in the hands of his father. The building of the body, mind, and spiritual awareness of the individual means a lot and is the measurement of one's work; thereby, one can enter into a happy life and enjoy the peaceful settings of a completed work in progress.

Productivity helps us as individuals to make positive marks in relation to a God in heaven who watches over us. By keeping a clean foundation and positive work efforts, we help one another prune the garden and pave roads to precious treasures here on earth. Christ spoke of being this bread from heaven that we can eat and was acknowledged by a sign in heaven that three wise men used to find him and his parents. During that time, children were being born, and Rome was expanding their territory throughout the Mediterranean coastline. The church, which was in Israel during that time, was being absorbed by the nationalism of Rome and taxation to finance the construction of an empire. Here I'll leave an excerpt from Matthew 2:12–21:

> And being warned of God in a dream
> that they should not return to Herod, they
> departed into their own country another
> way.
>
> And when they were departed,
> behold, the angel of the lord appeared to
> Joseph in a dream saying arise, and take
> the young child and his mother, and flee
> into Egypt, and be thou there until I bring
> thee word: for Herod will seek the young
> child to destroy him.

when he arose, he took the young
child and his mother by night and
departed into Egypt:

And was there until the death of
Herod: that it might be fulfilled which was
spoken of the lord by the prophet saying,
"Out of Egypt have I called my son."

Then Herod, when he saw that he was
mocked by the wise men, was exceeding
wroth, and sent forth, and slew all the children of Bethlehem, and in all the coast
thereof, from two years old and under,
according to the time which he had dili-
gently enquired of the wise men.

then was fulfilled that which was spoken by Jeremy the prophet saying,

In Rama was there a voice heard, lam-
entation, and weeping, and great mourn-
ing, Rachel weeping for her children, and
would not be comforted, because they
are not.

But when Herod was dead, behold
an angel of the lord appeareth in a dream
to Joseph in Egypt

Saying, Arise, and take the young
child and his mother, and go into the land
of Israel: for they are dead which sought
the young child's life.

and he arose, and took the young
child and his mother, and came into the
land of Israel. (Matthew 2:12–21)

## One Mature in the Faith

Taking the time to realize the young child's relationship
with the father surely helps us to see the structure and foun-

dation of a relationship with God not yet known to man. Being able to see in the spirit and discern the difference between his true father, "which art in heaven," and Joseph, his mother's husband's relationship with the son, which is Christ, may be the beginning of an honorable decent or spirit that teaches and nurtures the divine. First, the child was aware of the title and knew his job as a son of the father. History informs us of his holiness and presence throughout the book.

In this section, my task is to help reveal the mystery of his faith. Reading helps me see the maturity of Christ's mission, his life as a child from heaven versus the sin and corruption of this world, and its need for change. Learning to use the hands to escape folly and the corruption of sin while learning to walk in a path of righteousness for his name's sake is something I'm a little familiar with. Earlier, I spoke of elder Moses and his writing in the name of the father and how there is power in those names. For instance, Jehovah Rapha, our healer, may be the beginning of the secret languages one used to perform his miracle of salvation. In the teachings of Hebraic mysticism, the path is very important to the practitioner because of spiritual gifts. Gifts usually differ according to the faith of the individual or the blessing of the Holy Spirit. Some are prophets, while others teach and discern.

> And it came to pass, when Jesus had finished all these sayings, he said unto his disciples,
>
> Ye know that after two days is the feast of the Passover, and the son of man is betrayed to be crucified.
>
> Then assembled together the chief priests, and the scribes, and the elders of the people, unto the palace of the high priest, who as called Caiaphas.

and consulted that they might take Jesus by subtilty, and kill him.

But they said, "Not on the feast day, lest there be an uproar among the people.

Now when Jesus was in Bethanay, in the house of Simon the leper,

There came unto him a woman having an alabaster box of very precious ointment, and poured it on his head, as he sat at meat.

but when his disciples saw it, they had indignation, saying, to what purpose is this waste?

For this ointment might have been sold for much, and given to the poor.

When Jesus understood it, he said unto them, "Why trouble ye the woman?" For she hath wrought a good work upon me.

for you have the poor always with you: but me ye have not always.

For in that she hath poured this ointment on my body, she did it for my burial.

Verily I say unto you, Wheresoever this gospel shall be preached in the whole world, there shall also this, that this woman hath done, be told for a memorial of her.

Then one of the twelve, called Judas Iscariot, went unto the chief priests,

And said unto them, What will ye give me, and I will deliver him unto you? And they covenanted with him for thirty pieces of silver.

and from that time he sought opportunity to betray him. (Matthew 26)

# Drunken on the Blood of Christ

The gift of prophecy and those deemed worthy of the secret service, his trial, persecution, his death, and resurrection all play a very important role in the life of my Christian service as a Latter-day Saint. Some days are more difficult than others, yet the struggle continues. When I first entered this world, the caretakers and older ladies and gentlemen in my life were already here "working hard to prepare us youths for this day." My father enlisted in the United States Army while working two jobs as a mechanic, defined character and played a major role in my behavior as a youth. I lived with his mother while he worked hard raising his other two young men. Back then, I was in love with the role of being a grandson, working hard on my chores and career goals. Finding the word of God was very important to my education as a young man and really helped with the conduct of the simple while the more complex issues had their way.

Morals were always important, as well as the darker sayings of the elders around the house. Unfortunately, the war reared its head in the Middle East. I was called as a volunteer for sea service onboard USS Carl Vinson to the Persian Gulf area, where we as a unit set the "no fly zone." After returning home from deployment, I, as a technician, was called to christian service by the Holy Father YHWH to observe the Holy Scripture. Once I began to study, I was introduced to the gospel from Ethiopia. The Lord Emperor Haile Salassie's reign, Phillip, a disciple of Christ our Lord. Whose mission was confirmed by the deliverance of souls. A solid ministry of the gospel as a true nazarite, in accordance with the scrolls left by Solomon, the Emperor's grandfather. Years after my baptism in the Holy Spirit, we as a nation, experienced the terrorist attacks on Washington and the New York's World Trade Center.

I was called, as a technician, to restore the socioeconomic structure, fibers that hold the fabric of good business here in America. Here I have a collection of chapters written for the latter-day Saint's experience of an American author of native African American descent.

# A Book of Deadly Venom

A chapter based on surviving operation desert strike.

As a technician, I found grace in our Lord and Savior, Jesus Christ, shortly after the war. Training is hard work sometimes, suffering lack and hunger to nourish the temple. Strength in the fortress, the mind, body, and spirit of the individual are very important to the survival of the character. Excellence is the divine nature that propels one to greater heights. Before the war, I was a member of an engineering program here in Birmingham, Alabama, with a strong desire to study architecture. The good news is that I found God in Christ Jesus as my personal Lord and savior, whose message to me was, "Read and study his work."

The carpenter, the great physician, and the wonderful counselor's role as gods here in America have been excellent teachers and advisors to me as a disciple on this journey. As a soldier and a technician, my job was to repair the economy after the September 11 attack. While working the mainframe, I located this source of deadly venom that protects the body from harm and danger, a well rooted source that protects humanity, a freedom and liberty that safely guards the divinity of human rights. Christ is a life-supportive element that promotes good in the land; food, clothing, shelter, and the hand of the provider help support those fallen few that lay close to the foundation. Some call it the slab, where life gets hard. This piece is based on surviving enemy attacks I had to face while working on a social science engineering data program.

Winter winds that bite like cobras
A cup of baking soda
Another grain of sea salt
From the vault
Like fresh bread bought
This is a book of deadly venom
Like rhymes when they spit them
Trees when they split them
Some strike
Like light
In the dark night
Under the moon
So I consume the antidote
It burns
Like amino acid in my veins
No turning back
From the attack
Ninja toed assassins

## A closing chapter

## A book of red and black dragons

# Another Book of Deadly Venom

Welcome to this book of venom
The power of the tongue as it flickers
Becomes liquor
Like a quicker glimpse of things to come
The sacred seashore of my brother
My sister even knows the drill
A skill of deadly venom
A call to the deep
Who creeps through the darkness?
Over stones
Around bones
Into another man's zone
Looking for homestead
Like stolen bread
In the hands of a thief
From a coil position
It strikes
Undetected
Disrespected
By the Spirit
By the carnal mind
Tools to find a hidden motive
Before the python of poverty
Find my hands folded in comfort
Too soon to tell
The depth of the well
Or the path of the poison
I recognize the lies

And the disguise
Of the wise
That tempts to the path of death
Nothing left
Just respect for self
And the hidden mystery of scripture
The prescription
And pathogen of smooth words undisturbed
A good word in season
Like a grain of salt
To chase the poison
So I pause for a moment of silence
Violence
Like a hungry dog
Licking at stolen water
Or wounds before they close
Nose, ear, and throat swollen
Too hard to swallow
So I vomit these lines
To mastermind my patience
As candles burn
Lessons learned
Pages and paragraphs come to an end
Amen

# Black Dragon Blue Flame

A book of black phantoms
Ghost dog
Snake versus crane
Dragon tales
Master the Buddha
Mysteries of the inner self
This is a tale of black magic
Mysterious realm of the hidden Buddha
Master the art of ninjas
An assassin's tale

## A Book on Survival

Black magic
A closing chapter on recreation
A good source of human development

# Composition

Talents and tokens taken for granted, whether lost or stolen
Emerge from the deep
Like sunken treasure
From old pirate ships
Governed by lessons learned
Through the message of the Holy Script
Salvation is a free gift
Given to those who believe
This is another book of thieves
A passage on composition
Versus based on the level of competition
The race is not given to the swift
His holy word
Hard enough to fight
Steady enough to write
Evasive lines
That battle for my life
Like kites and keys
This is An American Anthem
A steady pace is the answer
From classwork to chores
More room out of doors
Locked with broken windows
And stolen legacies
Of history and malnutrition
So listen
To this composition
So that the shackle and chain

Of this old game we used to play
Won't leave us outside in the cold one day
This is a book of broken arrow
A chapter on the struggling male energy

# Beth

Wherewith shall a young man cleanse his way?
By taking heed thereto according to thy word.
With my whole heart have I sought thee.
O, let me not wander from thy commandments.
Thy word have I hid in mine heart that I may not sin against
thee.

# Concerning This Book

My goal here is to capture the essence of salvation through Christian service as a technician.

# Today Still Black in America

A conversation with my mother about school
Another day without God
It snowed last night
And I'm in college, studying
What it means to become a knight
The hardships
Of sunken ships
Through loose lips
And verbal struggles of the aged character
Who battle for the upper hand
Still black
And a young man
Here in America
The land of the free
And the home of the brave
Yet I struggle with the oppression
Of what once was a slave
Called a black man
When I'm brown as the earth in tone
Hard and soft, mud's skin and bone
A buffalo's soldier
In hard pursuit of lion's Rome
Afro pick for comb
Clinched fist, blood, skin, and bone
Deep zone
Like odes of shaman hymn in song
The flame and fire of God passing
Through clouds of holy smoke

Ghost-reaping dance of praise for hope
Lightening flashings hard in the heavens
To overthrow demonic revolt
Standing moon
Setting sun
Thunder's voice by choice of praise
Holy Ancient of Days
Prayer
Removes the yoke
Of high joke and scheme
Dopamine's travel
Fast as light
The infinite song of wisdom in her voice I heed
While greed is often mentioned
Struggling hard not to listen
A nerve is so precious in peace
Get a job, son, I need help around the home
When it's help that I seek all along
Thirty-five years I have lived
Seven from a bird's-eye view
Stressed by the summons of a call
Of the faithful few
On my way to Zion, I hope
To do what soldiers do
Standing on a wall
Between her might and her fall
An American anthem
As black as a panther
Mom, I have to suffer this call
"Don Quixote," she says
But, Mom, school is strength to stand this wall

# A song of the broken arrow

# Drunken Fist

A chapter on open-hand karate
Open hand
Closed fist
Laws of the supernatural
So I open my fist
Closed hand on my pick
To avoid the hell of nails
Lynch mobs
And hit squads
That rule the level
Eyes and lies
Like death
So I breathe
And cleave
To my path
And recognize
The Buddha
Reaching and teaching
Like wells of deep water
Law and order
For the slaughter
Of wicked men
Watching my breath and my step
Inside the box
Outside the box
Open the hand
To save a man
Close proximity

Not an enemy
Just confused
And booze
Drunken fist

A tale of the Broken Arrow, little sparrow on the block

A book of lost souls

Buddha's palm

# A Page on Justice

## Freedom, Liberty, and Justice for All

This piece is based on moral support and education, the foundation. Let us take a serious look at the forefathers, the founders, and documentation on the subject of American leadership, like the history of George Washington, the presiding officer, and the theory of democracy and the republic for which it stands. As a people, by the people, and for the people are three simplified element base forms that promote the individual, responsibility, and a quality focus on a lifestyle fit for service in this capitalistic society.

### The preamble to the constitution

Written by the framers of the Constitution of the United States of America.

We the people of the United States, in order to form a more perfect union, establish justice, insure domestic tranquility, provide for the common defense, promote general welfare, and secure the blessings of liberty to ourselves and our posterity, do

ordain and establish this constitution for
the United States of America.

We have rights as a nation of people united under the common cause of justice.

# Northeast Gate

Of the rising sun
Dawn's beauty
A chaste and rising star
Lovely lavender and violet sky
To behold thy loveliness
You have dove's eyes
Like unto the morning bird
You guard the gates of heaven
A city under sweet perfume
I wish the morning dew
Upon thy sandals
Before the rays of noon
Dressed in the quiet song
Of winter's wind
Gentle breeze of
Venus's mood
The awakening glory of the rising sun
The circuits of wind

# The Vermillion Bird

A song of songs
A book of genesis
The baker and the Cup Bearer...
I was resting by my bunk assignment
One night of mystic rain...
Bombarded by guest who seek the way.
Lost and in prisons' hold
One dark and dreary day....
Called to be a technician
In a cell of lumpy clay...
One lump of coal
While I pray...
Bread of Pharaoh
Made the baker's way...
Green light by the window
With the dew of night on my pillow...
Quite breezes that guard the way
Blinded by light on roads to Damascus
The light of the rising sun...
A fire in the sky...
That burns through page
Midnight scrolls
Of what destiny holds...

# Drawn Bow

Guardian of the gate...
Wounded skies
Arrow launched by crawling ground
Launched from the hollowed springs
Of holy ground
Holy round
Watcher of the morning fog
This log...
Guardian of the Most Holy Way
May thy paths be straight
Please observe thy way
Our safe stay
 Sacred Way
Why part Most High
Wounded sky
Drawn Bow...

# Purple Rain

Blue magic
Another book of black magic
Running this race between life and death
I have found the most wonderful gift, the mind of God
One must be very careful because of poison
Blue flames in the courtyard
Guarding the wall to Solomon's porch
Blackbirds fill the sky
Sage and thyme
A rose by the window
The heavens open
And paradise appears
Like a soothing peace
Ninja on the stairs
In a cloud of holy smoke
Guarding the way
Watch for poison
In arrows that fly
Another day in paradise
Protecting the soul from darkness
Blue ribbon, white dress
Purple rain
Pure magic
Was the smile
Through harsh realities of hardship and struggle
Blinded by moments in time
Like new wine in old skins
Drunken on the distance of days

In hopes of reaching a better tomorrow
The sorrow and pain of what remains open
Hoping that is well with us
Trust no tarnish, no rust my shield
For the yield of the fold is too cold
Intoxicated by the approach
Amazing Grace
Eleven before Heaven's Gate open
Be He Moth

# A closing chapter on black magic

# Purple rain

# The Book of Daniel

## The Book of God

*The siege by King Darius*

The free enterprise
Stacks of Persian rugs
Pure threads
Real camel hair
The Holy Spirit held the glory of God
A pure white and gold light
The radiance of the sun
That shines through righteousness
In those days, diet was of God
Food, the hand, and the provider
God's radiance shines as pure as a child's light
Untainted by the laws and decrees of man
Infinite knowledge and wisdom
He resides in a holy place
Lil' donkey
Was the word of God
"In the beginning" was the word
And the word was with God
The tree of life was happy fruit
That's before the slaughter came
Christ was the son of God
The son of man

God's Holy Word
We worshipped him in his glory and strength
Lucifer was the light bearer
Over the Heavenly chorus
He was displeased with man
The imperfections of life and death
No one knew Satan
Whether life or death
The devil was his works
His walk on the earth
A level of difficulty
Wrath and rage against the machine
A sword
A dragon
With two-thirds of God's congregation
Turned to confusion
The chaos and corruption of God the son
Many fell in those days
To death
The edge of the sword
Blood was on the earth
Daniel wouldn't eat during dinner
The peaches were in light corn syrup
We used to travel through the star gate with Natalis
A Great Sky Dragon

# The Book of Judges

In this section, I am attempting to relate the spiritual gift of God's Holy Word to man, the purity of the messenger and the hour of invocation and incarnation, and the calling of judges for the sacred duty of keeping his chosen people. First, I'll start with the thirteenth chapter, verses 1 to 5, pure from the womb, a blessing from God:

> And the children of Israel did evil again in the sight of the Lord; and the Lord delivered them in the hands of the philistines forty years.
>
> And there was a certain man of Zorah of the family of the Danites, whose name was Manoah; and his wife was barren, and bare not.
>
> And the angel of the Lord appeared unto the woman, and said unto her, behold now thou art barren and barest not: but thou shalt conceive, and bear a son.
>
> Now therefore beware, I pray thee, and drink not wine nor strong drink, and eat not any unclean thing:
>
> For, lo, thou shall conceive, and bear a son; and no razor shall come on his head: for the child shall be a Nazarite unto God from the womb: and he shall begin to deliver Israel out of the hands of the Philistines. (13:1–5)

Here, my goal is to expose the true nature of God in service and deed as a disciple of Christ and the revelation knowledge written and recorded in these scrolls of gratitude for Christian service in my life and the relationship of heavenly creatures with us earthly-bound citizens seeking our higher callings in truth and deed.

# The Book of Proverbs

## Written by King Solomon

Here, I will add an edge to the volume of these works by using the book of Proverbs to give the reader some idea of the depths retained in the Holy Scripture of the Hebrew Bible and my search for the holy grail, often referred to as wisdom in this collection of writings based on my salvation in Christ and a scroll through the King James Version of my English translation of the Bible I have at home.

First, I would like to explain how the search begins. Being called by the Holy Father as a technician, historian, and African American male native-born and located in the district of Birmingham, Alabama, I found grace in the gospel of Christ concerning the merciful blessings of human nature on a spiritual path one evening before sundown. Thereby I learned to follow my heart and listen deeply to the guidance of the Holy Spirit. In the beginning, I was called to order by the strict discipline of a disciple and the ability to relate through the gift of understanding. Murder was the case and the special assignment of the enemy. Here's the book of Proverbs:

> Proverbs of Solomon the son of David,
> king in Israel;
> To know wisdom and instruction; to
> perceive the words of understanding;

To receive the instruction of wisdom, justice, and judgment and equity;

To give subtilty to the simple, to the young man knowledge and discretion.

A wise man will hear, and will increase in learning; and a man of understanding shall attain unto wise counsels:

To understand a proverb; and the interpretation; the words of the wise, and their dark sayings.

The fear of the Lord is the beginning of knowledge: but fools despise wisdom and instruction.

My son, hear the instruction of thy father, and forsake not the law of thy mother:

For they shall be an ornament of grace unto thy head, and chains about thy neck.

My son, if sinners entice thee, consent thou not.

If they say, come with us, let us lay wait for blood, let us lurk privily for the innocent without cause:

let us swallow them up alive as the grave; and whole, as those that go down into the pit:

we shall find all precious substance; we shall fill our houses with spoil:

Cast in thy lot among us; let us all have one purse. (Proverbs 1:1–14)

It has brought me to "this point of no return." I wish there was more that I could tell you, but too much is not enough, and all the reading in the world won't change the world unless we make a difference. So hold fast to the teachings of the Holy Bible because it is important that you are acceptable in the presence of glory, and on the day of atonement, all will be well with you.

# The First Book of Samuel 1—13

*In attempts to bridge the gap of time and prepare a kingdom for the return of an almighty*

Now there was a certain man of Ramathaim-zophim, of mount Ephraim, and his name was Elkanah, the son of Jeroham, the son of Elihu, the son of Tohu, the son of zuph, an Ephrathite:

And he had two wives; the name of the one was Hannah, and the name of the other Peninnah: and Peninnah had children, but Hannah had no children.

And this man went up out of his city yearly to worship and to sacrifice unto the Lord of hosts in Shiloh: And the two sons of Eli, Hophni and Phinehas, the priest of the lord, were there.

And when the time was that Elkanah offered, he gave to Peninnah his wife, and to all her sons and daughters, portions:

But unto Hannah he gave a worthy portion; for he loved Hannah: but the Lord had shut up her womb.

And her adversary also provoked her sore, for to make her fret, because the Lord had shut up her womb.

And as he did so year by year, when she went up to the house of the Lord, so she provoked her; therefore she wept and did not eat.

Then said Elkanah her husband to her, Hannah why weepest thou? And why eatest thou not? And why is thy heart grieved? Am not I better to thee than ten sons?

so Hannah rose up after they had eaten in Shiloh, and after they had drunk. Now Eli the priest sat upon a seat by a post of the temple of the Lord.

And she was in bitterness of soul, and prayed unto the Lord, and wept sore.

And she vowed a vow, and said, o Lord of Host, if thou wilt indeed look upon the affliction of thine handmaid, and remember me, and not forget thine handmaid, but wilt give unto thine handmaid a man child, then I will give him unto the Lord all the days of his life, and there shall no razor come upon his head.

And it came to pass, as she continued praying before the Lord, that Eli marked her mouth.

Now Hannah, she spake in her heart; only her lips moved, but her voice was not heard: therefore Eli thought she had been drunken.

# The Raven

Black as the knight is young
She sits in my window
Rap, rap, rapping
In our native tongue
With the wingspan
Of saved wow man
She drops a buttered roll
Dear Raven
Outside of my broken window

# The Red Dragon

## "Red Rum"

## Another Book of Deadly Venom

A book of tender mercies
A book of deadly venom
A crawl before my first step
Red rum on their breath
Red eyes and cold lies
Even hard truths
Since my youth
Cool tails with fresh hair and nails
Was a thing before bling
Now I'm a soldier
Where it's colder
Outside of closed doors
Locked even
Crops even
Burn on a block
Where cotton pickers died
Watch my step
Before death seizes me cold
Mainline venom
A book of the God's
A stroll through the garden

A day before darkness
The harken of a hearty heartbeat
For one who walks the streets
Without heat
To the beat of a different drum
Red rum

In this chapter, Broken Arrow is an ex-naval aviation technician who has been called by the Holy One of Israel (the Holy Father YHWH) to complete a faithful task of surveying the aftermath of the September 11 attack on the World Trade Center. In the process, his eyes open to the danger of a collapsing society in need of care and fortification. As a history student and former member of the American Institute of Architects, he decides to repair the fallen society and declares it holy ground by using the office of planning and design to restore the fallen communities. Using a scale model home and recycled brick, the technician tries his hand at making it to the Alabama Museum of Art until further notice. In the process, the skilled technician witnesses a storm that reveals a hidden dragon, the red tail of a hidden dragon, and the arrow smith.

# The Wall

## The Stairs to Heaven's Gate

Here, in this piece, using the Holy Scripture, I have made an attempt to capture the essence of the divine journey promised to us by Christ Jesus, Lord and Savior, of this world and the world to come. This block of light-sentenced fragments have been composed to enlighten the readers concerning the faith and the truth of our Lord's promise of salvation to those who come to him for the help of their soul's deliverance unto life everlasting in a sanctuary of peace, love, liberty, and happiness forevermore abundantly.

> The way seems long and hard
> One must be upright with others
> Black and white issues
> Skin tissue
> Like pure white
> And clean browns
> A town of two gold
> With twofold
> Many have died
> In search for what only heaven knows
> It glows
> The skin
> Of righteous men
> By the wall

There's a gate
Beyond the gate
Some stairs
A tree
That bears fruit
Was some juice
A couple of angels
With swift wings
A mixture of cooling elements
One day
And two knights

A book of Lords
The rook

# War Face

## The Wagon Wheel of My Chariot

A defensive technique
Shadowboxing dawn
For the price of peace
Cracks in the veil
Reveals a glimpse of light
In the concrete
An instrumental
Paper and pencil
Space and time
So I'm on the grind
Chopping tall pines, no cedar
Winter winds
No heater
Silence the virtue
Bushido
The art of chopping wood

# The Dust of the Earth

## The green lantern

The wagon wheels of my chariot
Rolling Thunder through
The dusty plains of what remains sacred
Hoping that all is well
Bumped by bravery
Challenged by might
My chariot ride
Through the night
A green lantern
The race is not given to the swift
Enough grace to win a race
Wet roads and shaman odes
Hymn the rim
Low profile
Hard to pinpoint victory
My job is history
What's behind in the rhythm of one's might
Apocalyptic horses
Still riding thunder...
Blue magic
Cloudy white sky dragon
No rain
Just the dust of the earth...

# Heaven's Glory

Angelic swords
Might
Young knight
Angels fly
There are reasons why
Distressed
Yet dressed for combat
Minds clothed in righteousness, for their sakes
It's better to be blessed
In spite of
When wrong is forced
Like vials of hatred
Are poured to misplace heaven's scent
And the descent of the cruel
Becomes fuel for hell's fire
Like impoverished nations
And notions about potions
Which battle against plagues of sickness
That usually gives rise to chaos
The rooftop
Peace
In search for the word of God
In its timely essence
Exalted on a mountaintop
To relight the surface
The core
The carbon of combustion mingles with the falling rain
Soil again

To the ashes from which it rose
Like the flight of the phoenix
Drunken in utterance
When the name of what remains
Can be tamed into existence
Through the knowledge of its composition
No longer in competition
Only clay pots
No spots to taint the living episodes
Of those earthen vessels composed
Yet choose for a greater work than pride
Although the strength that resides
Remains a holy source, of course
Like cooling streams
Of evening dawn
When the sunrays return
To the intimate feelings of the flesh
Soulstress, goddess
When or if the almighty was the universe that held us
Until someone beheld us
Then pain would only last for corruptible moments in time
No matter how long the journey may take
For heaven's sake
A narrow road
Understanding that hell is only an episode
Downtrodden through the forgotten
Or unknown
Goodness and mercy follow the merciful
And mercy was triumphant over judgment
While the meek inherit the earth
Often shades of green in tone
When clean in zone
And right is wrong

Then who belongs in thy holy place
I wish you grace
In an amazing place where the gods play
A game of salvation

# Heaven's Scent

# Another book by Broken Arrow

# Concerning the Kingdom of God

# The Grand Duchess

## A Missing Chapter

Here in this scroll,

I am attempting to perform the miracle of education reform. By clothing the students with quality essence, a subject concerning class and uniformity to promote education and performance helps intensify the learning experience. The purpose is to eliminate a certain area of peer pressure. Personally, I believe that early childhood development is centered on teaching and a foundation knowledge of the curriculum offered to the students. Similar to a degree plan, one should be comfortable in the learning experience to master the subject for a better education. For example, the higher education subject for shaping and grooming is similar to the branch or quality education for a struggling student who decides to stop after graduation for trade or family responsibilities. I also believe that centering a student's performance based upon a nation's need for loyal participants in a responsible call of duty as young men and women will help prevent crime and unemployment based on education on the subject.

Try looking into the subject and experience the topic of programming and its effects on early childhood development. Personally, I think programming is effective and deserves to be structured based on our need as a people to survive the destructive elements that can cause a house value to decline. Change is a factor in our lives that may need some attention. Some of the titles in this book are written in old English script. The purpose is for a closer look into the fourteenth- and fifteenth-century fox that has kept a house strong and productive. Try looking into the subject so we, as a people, can experience the American dream and not Lose this great country due to corruption, or the misfortune of bad leadership, or lack of quality service.

The Bread of Life

# The Genesis

*The first book of Moses*
*A chapter by Broken Arrow*
In the beginning, darkness was the light
Upon the face of the deep
A blind knight
The void of insight
Wisdom was the voice of the deep
Silence was neat
Thereby one creeps
Sometimes crawl
Behind this wall
In a position to prevent destruction
With construction
On paper with pen
Mighty like a lost sword
Was the void
A razor-sharp edge
A pledge
To deliver this peace
Outpoured on the streets
To bind a beast
Sharp arrows
From the quiver
To the liver
Delivered a blow
Like unto the first trumpet sound
When he fell
It shook the ground

Like the crown of great kings.

## A *closing* chapter of dragon's blood

A drip from his dagger on wax

## A book of holy angels

# The Fortress

*This piece is based on strength and human capability.*

Eyes opening to the rising of the sun
Challenged
The evening comes
A book of styles and forms
Nothing is left undone
Water to quench the thirst
In the rays of the golden sun

## A book of Broken Arrow

## Little sparrow on the roof

# Repentance

The sentence of what my steps have started...
A party...
Arrayed in fine linen...
A heavenly host...

# Red Sea Scrolls

*The ships of Sheba's men from the tents of Kadar*

Long before the days of Egypt began
I had an architect friend
Stones from mud we would blend
In a world free from sin
Strong woods from cedar, we would bend
To float the water
Time and time again
Strong herbs and spice
She would send
Long before the days of Solomon
My friend
One hundred men
Bags of gold nuggets
Emeralds
No rubies for them
No rubies until the days of Solomon
They sold men
Boatloads
For fish and rare skin
No rubies for them
Until the days of Solomon
Strong branches of honey
Apricots for blend
Strong sugarcane, bark, and molasses
Spice, ale, and skin
We built a temple of God

In the days back then
Arabian scrolls
Aladdin's den
Magic carpets we bought from them
With a gold and emerald green ring
Back then, before they called one king
Together we ate gator and crock for a swim
Climbed mountains
To the south beach
Summoned Zulu Nation for the gem of thread
Gazelle skins and golden beads for dread
No rubies, no rubies, no rubies of red
Just gold and green emeralds
For exotic plants and herbs of sage
From the days of Eden
The gardens grove
Long before we planted the lotus gardens of Thebes
We rode horse and chariot
To the shores to meet Ali Bubba
And his forty thieves
To gather Persian gold tobacco leaves
Pulling spliffs of smoke
In American trees
In the days of harvest
Like hives of bees
We traveled the seas
Long before the Greeks entered the gateway of Thebes
We had a throne
Our home
A porch of gees
Gates of eights and Geez
We wrapped our dead in bark from forest trees
Scented in saps of pine
Inscriptions of their lives
To bless the essence
Long before dead bodies became someone's blessing

Green emeralds and gold
No rubies, no rubies until Solomon comes
Under the tents of Kadar
Where we drank our spiced rum
And played the drum
Pearls from the Mediterranean
We played the drums for noon
For Asonya, goddess of the moon
Young lions on the plane
In the days of the open planes
Climbing the mountains of Zion
For worship and praise
Together in song and dance
We would softly summon the ancient of days
Rubies for Solomon
The son of Dave
He worshiped the lord through onyx
And praise
High in the heavens
The ancient days
Ships of Zebulon
Quick to Zebulon's gateway
"Rubies for Solomon," Sheba would say
Under the tents of Kadar
The young warriors would play
No rubies of red
Just emeralds and gold to heal our earth, I say

# A song from broken arrow

# Queen Isabella

## The Death of a Thousand Lords

After the cocaine epidemic, thousands of young men found profit in the product. Hustling became big, and the American dream was no longer just a dream but something tangible.

Something they could reach...
With the right amount of hustle and patience,
    money became a fluent enterprise...
Long before the powder was cooked...
A book opened...
Hustling in the seventies was relevant, it seemed...
With stipulations, young males faced in African
    American communities, English, and all...
Who really understood this, Lord...
Wrestling with civil rights and culture,
    decisions had to be made...
And the dope had already been cut...
Dope geez, the speed of the Elohim, his heart
    and soul and all, why shape it right...
Well, something went wrong...
A civilization underwater...
Dope in a process...
who could measure such depth in man's
    freedom and development...

In a country where freedom and enterprise
        support lavish living...
The product, the supply, and the demand...
The freedom, the cool of the night, no watch
        tower or mad watchmen...
Seizing life by the tale, it seemed...
The man and the science, all in their hands...
It made life seem so much easier...
To love a place as beautiful as the raw nature
        of America was far from their realities...
Trapped in a society where money exchanges
        for a product deeper entrenched into
        a shell of deceptive design...
The search for manhood became relevant...
Brother Roy Johnson understood this...
A perfect time to capitalize on their need...
Quality living, he realized, was better in the end...
A place where people could go and live this dream...
This dream without the harsh realities of poverty...
Blessed is the man who understood this...
He focused hard on school studies, his history,
        and the start of this whole drama...
He knew Odessa and the moves he made...
As a friend, he hoped that someday the people
        would understand that education wasn't
        a bad word... Just understand...
"Tools are important," he would always mention...
His grandfather was a strong farmer who
        worked hard every day of their life...
Except on the Sabbath...
He would always mention, "That day belongs to God..."
Roy respected that...
After all, for some weeks it was his only rest...
People may depend on you was something his
        grandfather would always mention...
He understood...

After the lobster farm, having a few bucks
        to spare meant a lot to him...
His life...
After finishing law school, he made his
        move toward real estate...
Buying land was always important to him...
One day while farming yams, his grandfather
        mentioned getting the soil underneath his feet...
Digging deep for what's important to
        him and others in life...
Visions of the wagon ride to mobile with Emma,
        Elizabeth, and Odessa always would run
        through his mind during Sabbath's rest...
After the trip to Mobile, Odessa found a raw soul...
It took him so fast backward...
He never really wanted to return to the society
        that his forefathers had fought for...
He found the amazon and Spanish gold...
After spending years in the apothecary art of crushing
        herbs for the oil of smoke and fire, he wanted more...
Deep into the heart of the jungle, money became
        power, and so was the product...
After meeting with Pierre, the coco smith...
Crushing nutmegs and cocoa beans
        paid its share of bills...
After the marriage to Elizabeth...
She was very fond of baking, a country girl
        from the heart of Alabama...
They made pies and dealt in raw materials,
        fresh herbs, and spice...
Brazilian brownies with Brazil nuts, fresh
        caramels, and vanilla...
Strong rums and brandy...
Fresh tobacco products...
Odessa was never really fond of help...

After Isabella was born, Odessa separated from the
        coffee shop to operate free enterprise...
Inner city, blues and jazz, liquor and hustle...
Always fast and strictly business...
Move like a serpent, killer bee, long-haired
        locust, a stick and move hustle...
He knew the plagues, he knew the horse,
        and he knew the seals...
"True buffalo soldier," he called her...
He thought about Roy every now and then...
After all, that's how he met Elizabeth...
Dealing in raw soul honey and herbs...
He made millions...
It wasn't easy...
It took every moment of his time...
A constant hustle...
He knew the man and never talked to
        the man for over a minute...
After all, his time was precious to him...
No bullshit was his first wrath...
Later, he realized something was about
        to go sour, wrong even...
At that time, his daughter had just turned seven...
He thought what could be more precious
        than returning home to spend quality
        time as a teacher to his youth...
But the product was already on the market...
The demand was greater than the hustle...
Bigger packs, another call, another city,
        and another "cat slim..."
He knew the grim reaper...
The pain of spending time away from his family...
Back in Brazil, around the coffee shop...
Good tidings, a clean hustle...
Over in the states, the game was going sour...

Cuts and shit dealing, little petty hustle,
        greed, want, and the demand...
Pure supply was his truth, his horse, his Lord and Savior...
After all, he had a daughter to raise...
He remembered Roy and Emma, their ride to Mobile,
        the boat ride to Brazil, and his first encounter
        with Pierre, how well life had been...
A dollar was nothing but something
        everybody seemed to need...
He enrolled Isabella in a Methodist academy after
        remembering this conversation with Roy about the
        history of America and Brother Frederick Douglass...
And Brother Abraham Lincoln's struggle
        with the freedom riders...
After the nation split and was reunited
        under his command...
He figured, "Well, let her serve after she has learned..."
Odessa decided to step out of the business...
Darkness reared its head in the death
        of a thousand lords...
He watched in the distance as street wars
        and crime became passion...
For the love of money...
"The Pale Horse of Death," he called it...
He remembered the cold slither of the tongue...
He knew the grim reaper...
After all, harvest was his thing...
Usually, Pierre kept the fields while Odessa rode...
The hives, the honey, the spice, and dried
        peppers crushed into powders...
Raw cinnamons, creams, fresh pie, trips to New York,
        Philly, cream cheese, and raw enterprise...
Pure flames, fresh raw bark for coal,
        scents of juniper and musk...
Pure fine gold...

Elizabeth's lamp at night by the coffee table
        and nightstand, where she took care of
        overhead and read to Isabella…
Out by the pool, years by the fire, they silently
        watched the death of a thousand lords…
Nights over the bay, the gulf would get cold and windy…
She would read to Isabella…
Pierre's wife took over the coffee shop…
After Isabella turned seven, they moved back
        to an estate in North Alabama…
With a spiral staircase that led back to the
        staircase into the dining area and sofa near
        the French doors that lead to the pool…
Odessa bought a Bentley…
He drove Isabella to school for ten years in that Bentley…
Life around the inner city began to decline…
After all, a crack had found its way into the foundation…
He knew the pale horse and didn't really
        want to get involved…
He saw the bitterness of being away from
        what was more important…

# Isabella Meets Raphael

One day at school, after the young lords had
        finished a soccer game at state...
A young player by the name of Raphael Redwine of
        Dunmore stumbled upon Isabella, watching as they
        returned walking towards the morning session...
After morning prayer, a private affair...
They went to morning session where the dean of
        students would drill yesterday before tomorrow...
The school rarely accepts anything less
        than perfect achievement...
"Bs" were considered and referred to as
        inferior by most students...
Isabella loved school...
She rarely looked at the young men because she was
        a young lady who was loved by her parents...
It was something about the young man's socks
        and loafers that caught her attention...
While passing, he offers a long stem rose after tradition...
Her mother and father often brought her flowers...
It pleased her...
*It was of God*, she thought, knew even
        that one must be watching...
Her father was a pure Nazarite and knew the scripture...
"His heed is most high," she would often consider...
Isabella loved school...
Her favorite book was *Esther a Queen in Persia*...
How wonderful it would be to enjoy queen for a night...
A young knight even she thought...

The wind blew and revealed his wing…
A whisper in the wind spoke, saying,
        "Keep him, he is yours…"
She knew in her heart somewhere that
        she was a keeper of souls…
Her duty, as a child of God, for the first time,
        began to totally make sense…
That night she wrote a twelve-page letter explaining how
        the gods spoke concerning their mission and how he
        was an angel assigned to her for a divine purpose…
In the letter, she asked him did he know…
She explained how it was her job to keep him…
She wrote concerning the long road to Bessemer…
The Bessemer road has a lot to do with
        the reality of the mission…
Often young hearts and minds can corrupt their peers,
        not realizing the importance of true faith…
Who or what does he believe in, heaven or hell…
How most of her life, her father and mother were her
        best friends but wasn't much time for play…
Because of tasks and proper business management…
She spoke about the cold of the knight…
She spoke concerning how he could soar
        and reach God if he tried…
On her way to school the next morning, her father asked
        her a few questions concerning the fellow…
She wondered a little, but he often talks to God in riddle…

# Isabella's invitation to the Dunmore Estate…

# Mecca

A place of prayer and worship
A book of black jewels
The panther and the prince
Tiger style
Way down in the jungle, deep
I was a prince
Paving concrete
From a Greco-Roman scroll
With a scroll
And a scale
Searching for a place for souls to dwell
A hidden porch
With couches made of brass
To rest one's bag
A touch of class
A fountain of water
To shower the past
A closing chapter of rest
Hidden in the jungle, deep
A place where tigers creep

## A book of broken arrow

# Dragon Fruit

Enter the dragon
A place where the gods play
Good deeds
Some most high
Taking chances
Games that are godly
Sophisticated wordplay
Soft-spoken style
Like mystic rain
That falls
Halls of judgment
Cloudy sky
Two tigers
Slow stroll
Windy, it seems
This morning I saw the moon
Instead of the sun
Another blue moon
Five in two months
Dragon fruit
She must be sleeping
The sky is weeping
The first sign of spring
I'm broken arrow
Little sparrow on the roof

## A book of rain

# A Book of Holy Angels

A book of the living
Another book of dragon's blood
Starstruck
By the light
Sword and shield
For the yield of the fold
Cold
Windy
Another book of rain
Arrows that fall
From the heavens above
Crash against the earth
Turf wars
Like burrowed hallows
For haloes
And pesos
Flood the ground
In this one town
Showdowns at high noon
In a valley of dry bones
Where the dead
Wear chrome
Lost battles
And wars
Frozen
Because of the chosen
Heroes and heroines
That departs

The faith
For a taste
Of cracked helmets
And broken swords
Of gods
That chose the battle
While horses
Of calvary
Joust for justice
With just this
Pen of a ready writer

# A book of broken arrow

# This Queen

Back when God was young
And immortality was a song of praise
A song we sang each day
To realize the depth of God
An illuminated heart song
Golden, in a way
As golden as the blazing sun rays that protect her glory
Since the beginning of time
Like the fallen plums, this one
The ants had burrowed deep holes into the core
Palm branches like the wings of the wind
As berries in spring glasses
Like grains of sand in an hourglass
As they pass
This concerns a golden grail
Simply a figure of speech
To teach
To refuse any unjust
Trust, a shining shield
No tarnish, no rust
A faith in God
No hurry, no rush
A thousand years
A thousand lines
A thousand soldiers
Behold this dime
A helmet of salvation
A golden belt for truth

She was God in glory
They were in line, over a thousand too
The honey was slim
The bees poured plenty
Acres were grand
Over a thousand and twenty
Dried fruits and pure water
Sweat had a fuel
Hard work, we entertained
For our fortune and fame
A holy name
Dirt was a shame
Ascending crystal stairs had a cream
Crystal and cream
Long journeys of awakenings and dreams
For the word of God was a thing
A book
I looked
And the pages had life
A fruit, a tree, and a knife
A knife?
This Queen
Holy Torah
She broiled fish with celery and purple onion with steam
A little salt
A little pepper
She offered me a look
This queen of heaven
Guarding a nation
With season and scepter
By her side was Lord
Few have left her
A man's home is his castle
A thousand yards
A thousand lords

# 21<sup>st</sup> Century Fox

This piece is based on a social science overview and the problems we have to face in society as a people united for liberty, freedom, and justice for us all.

> Winter winds
> That blow against the den
> Just a phase
> Or a season
> One must face
> In this place of opportunity
> Some communities are in shambles, it seems
> The American dream
> And a team
> That fulfills the promise of shelter
> To protect us from cold weather
> A warm cup
> That'll heat things up
> Property price and protection
> In this resurrection
> To heal the soul
> Of the fallen few
> Written to guard the gentry
> In this twentieth century
> Like young lords of the elementary
> We witnessed a promised land
> Promise to guard her soul against the cold
> A technique
> A method

A hand
Good man
Before the curtains close

# Summer Rain

A chapter on crucial concepts
Pain and struggle
Broken hearts
And player cards
All have their part
In this summer's rain
The grass grows tall
Against the wall
While the halls of justice
Remain open
Like the windows in heaven
Opening
Like the eyes on a newborn babe
To this world
And the problems we have to face
Race for solutions
Before the pollution
Of poisoned minds
Mislead the blind
And hells become havens
Through neglect and foolish pride
The ride and race
Is not given to the swift
What a gift
This world
You and I
Like protons
And positive charges

In the sky
Lightning strikes the ground
And thunder resounds
Rumbling between the heavens and the earth
Turf, not taken for granted
But taken for treasured time
Tall pines broken
By heavy winds
Leave a scent
While some bent
Not broken
Leaves us the strength to endure

# A closing chapter

# A book by Broken Arrow

# A chapter based on preserving the union

# Broken Arrow

# About the Author

Greetings,

Dear readers, my purpose for writing this book is based on a turn-of-the-century evaluation of a system designed for the people and by the people to uphold justice, peace, and liberty for all of mankind living here in America and abroad to provide and restore a safe haven for those who believe in God and his calling to the salvation of mankind.

The foundation of a union in need of restoration and the hospitality of a people who know the way are two major factors that have inspired me to write this message to the people. I would like to refer to this sacred call of duty as post-9/11 documentation based on some minor problems we face as American citizens from a native point of view.

Sometimes war rises, and we, as enlightened beings, have our sacred calling to promote justice and peace to restore a foundation torn by drugs and crime in some communities while neglected in others. To promote quality living standards and capture the American dream that was the original plan of the forefathers and drafters who designed the original format of this blessed land of opportunity. Thanks for your support; may peace be with you.

www.ingramcontent.com/pod-product-compliance
Lightning Source LLC
Chambersburg PA
CBHW031635170726

47990CB00017B/1098